Saving Graces

First published by Parragon in 2011

Parragon
Queen Street House
4 Queen Street
Bath BA1 1HE, UK

Copyright © Parragon Books Ltd 2011
Design by Pink Creative Ltd

ISBN: 978-1-4454-3852-8

Printed in China

Saving
Graces

a collection of inspirational thoughts and images

Bath · New York · Singapore · Hong Kong · Cologne · Delhi
Melbourne · Amsterdam · Johannesburg · Auckland · Shenzhen

Don't **wait** for the Last **Judgment**. It happens **every** day.

Albert Camus

Faith is a living, daring confidence in God's grace, so sure and certain that a man could stake his life on it a thousand times.

Martin Luther

Our greatest glory
is not in never falling
but in rising every
time we fall.

Confucius

A man travels the world over in search of what he needs and returns home to find it.

George Moore

In a gentle way,
you can shake
the world.

Mahatma Ghandi

Nothing in life is to be feared. It is only to be understood.

Marie Curie

To **know**
the road **ahead,**
ask those coming **back.**

Chinese Proverb

To me, every hour
of the day and night
is an unspeakably
perfect miracle.

Walt Whitman

Give light
and people will
find the way.

Ella Baker

As we struggle

to make sense

of things, life looks

on in repose.

Anonymous

Don't **cry** because it's over.
Smile because it happened.

Dr. Seuss

In the middle
of difficulty
lies opportunity.

Albert Einstein

Do not **wait** for
your ship to come in -
swim out to it.

Anonymous

It's always
too early
to quit.

Norman Vincent Peale

What **matters** is not
the **idea** a man holds,
but the **depth** at
which he holds it.

Ezra Pound

Most men pursue pleasure with such breathless haste that they hurry past it.

Søren Kierkegaard

Stand at the crossroads, and look, and ask for the ancient paths, where the good way is and walk in it, and you will find rest for your souls.

Jeremiah 6:16

Fear makes the wolf bigger than he is.

German Proverb

Faith is taking the first step
even when you don't see
the whole staircase.

Martin Luther King Jr.

Gratitude is the fairest blossom which springs from the soul.

Henry Ward Beecher

A man who doesn't **trust** himself can never truly trust anyone else.

Cardinal de Retz

Resolve to be thyself;
and know that he who finds
himself, loses his misery.

Matthew Arnold

Hope is a waking dream.

Aristotle

It is never too late
to be what you might
have been.

George Eliot

Yesterday is history.

Tomorrow is a mystery.

And today? Today is a gift.

That's why we call it

the present.

Babatunde Olatunji

Fear knocked at the door.
Faith answered.

And lo, no one was there.

Anonymous

Do not seek to follow in the footsteps of the wise. Seek what they sought.

Matsuo Basho

Learn as if you were

going to live forever.

Live as if you were

going to die tomorrow.

Mahatma Gandhi

If you can find a path

with no obstacles,

it probably doesn't lead

anywhere.

Frank A. Clark

Look at everything as though
you were seeing it either for the
first or last time.

Betty Smith

The best way to succeed in life is to act on the advice we give to others.

Anonymous

It is a good divine
that follows his own
instructions.

William Shakespeare

It's not what you
look at that matters,
it's what you **see**.

Henry David Thoreau

The way to gain a **good** reputation, is to endeavour to be what you **desire** to appear.

Socrates

A problem is a chance
for you to do your best.

Duke Ellington

A man can be
destroyed
but not defeated.

Ernest Hemingway

Do what you can, with what you have, where you are.

Theodore Roosevelt

To live is the rarest

thing in the world.

Most people exist,

that's all.

Oscar Wilde

The essence of pleasure is

spontaneity.

Germaine Greer

No snowflake
ever falls in the
wrong place.

Zen

Reason is our soul's left hand,
Faith her right.

John Donne

Man is a being in search of meaning.

Plato

The awareness of our
strength
makes us
modest.

Paul Cézanne

Faith is a living, daring confidence in God's grace, so sure and certain that a man could stake his life on it a thousand times.

Martin Luther

God will never give you any problems that he thinks you can't solve.

Og Mandino

Have a heart that never hardens, a temper that never tires, a touch that never hurts.

Charles Dickens

Picture credits

p4-5 © Luis Mariano González/Getty; p6-7 © Altrendo Images/Getty; p8-9 © Julie Rideout/Getty; p10-11 © Frank Gaglione/Getty; p12-13 © Andy Roberts/Getty; p14-15 © John K. Goodman/Getty; p16-17 © Ian Horne/Getty; p18-19 Gino Maccanti/Getty; p20-21 © Nick Dolding/Getty; p22-23 © C.Dollan/Getty; p24-25 © Fred Froese/Getty; p26-27 © Brian Lawrence/Getty; p28-29 © Grant Faint/Getty; p30-31 © Gallo Images-Hein von Horste/Getty; p32-33 © Lawren/Getty;p34-35 © Damian Hock/Getty; p36-37 © Radius Images/Getty; p38-39 © Gerlinde Hofmann/Getty; p40-41 © Ian Cumming/Getty; p42-43 © Harald Sund/Getty; p44-45 © Kathy Collins/Getty; p46-47 © Rémi Carreiro/Getty; p48-49 © Frank Gaglione/Getty; p50-51 © Juzant/Getty; p52-53 © Sabine Lubenow/Getty; p54-55 © Gerald Majumdar/Getty; p56-57 © Tiina & Geir/Getty; p58-59 © Dave Shafer/Getty; p60-61 © Chip Forelli/Getty; p62-63 © Jean-Paul Nacivet/Getty; p64-65 © Edwin H. Beckenbach/Getty; p66-67 © David Aaron Troy/Getty; p68-69 © Andrew Lockie/Getty; p70-71 © Gary Yeowell/Getty; p72-73 © Image Source/Getty; p74-75 © Irene Lamprakou/Getty; p76-77 © Plattform/Getty; p78-79 © Joseph Mule/Getty; p80-81 © Ulf Boettcher/Getty; p82-83 © Maarten Wouters/Getty; p84-85 © Jorg Greuel/Getty; p86-87 © Nivek Neslo/Getty; p88-89 Michael Melford/Getty; p90-91 © David Henderson/Getty; p92-93 © Michael Duva/Getty; p94-95 © Vsevolod Vlasenko/Getty.